A GIFT FOR:

_____

FROM:

_____

FRESH-CUT
Flowers
FOR
MY MOM

GIFT BOOKS
from Hallmark

BOK 4087

COUNTRYMAN

Compiled and edited by Terri Gibbs.

Designed by Garborg Design Works, Minneapolis, Minnesota

Photos by Lisa Garborg

www.hallmark.com
www.thomasnelson.com

ISBN: 1-4041-0008-3

Printed and bound in China.

Hundreds of dewdrops to greet the dawn,
Hundreds of bees in the purple clover,
Hundreds of butterflies on the lawn,
But only one mother the wide world over.

GEORGE COOPER

Lessons learned at mother's knee last through life.

LAURA INGALLS WILDER

Well, at least the ones you remember. But it's funny how they keep popping up now and then. Just when you need them the most.

Where else can you go to find
comfort, acceptance, forgiveness,
encouragement, praise, and
consolation . . . all in one hug?

Mother is the name for
God in the lips and
hearts of children.

WILLIAM THACKERAY

You respect me enough to be truthful, even when it is painful and unpleasant. I don't usually say so, but I appreciate it.

Mom is a tough friend. I know she is going to be honest with me.

ROBERT ELDRIDGE

The mother is and must be,
whether she knows it or not, the
greatest, strongest, and most
lasting teacher her children have.

HANNAH WHITALL SMITH

*Thanks for standing true to your
own ideas and convictions. It
has helped me be true to mine.*

Love is, above all,

the gift of oneself.

JEAN ANOUILH

God gives us friends—

and that means much;

but far above all others,

the greatest of His gifts

to earth was when He

thought of mothers.

ANONYMOUS

*It is a gift that lasts
through all our days.*

One mother achieves more
than a hundred teachers.

YIDDISH PROVERB

Actually, I think
you achieved more
in my life than any
single teacher
I ever had.

14

How comforting to think of the love
that always fills a mother's heart
and spills over into the home.

Love begins at home.

MOTHER TERESA

16

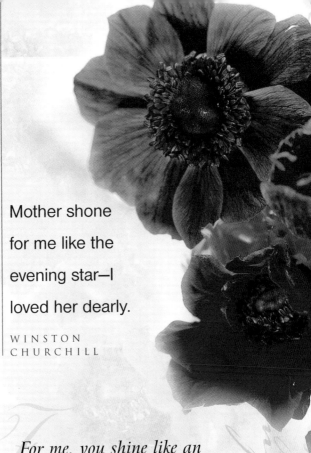

Mother shone
for me like the
evening star—I
loved her dearly.

WINSTON
CHURCHILL

For me, you shine like an
entire star-filled sky glowing
with a golden moon.

Who ran to help me when I fell,

And would some pretty story tell,

Or kiss the place to make it well?

My Mother.

ANNE TAYLOR

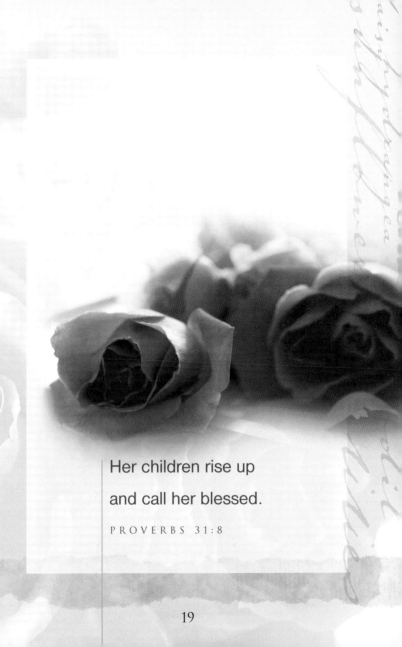

Her children rise up

and call her blessed.

PROVERBS 31:8

19

Who can ever measure

the benefit of a

mother's inspiration?

CHARLES R. SWINDOLL

I owe heaven an
unpayable debt for giving
me a God-fearing mother.

21

There is no friendship, no love, like that of the parent for the child.

HENRY WARD BEECHER

More than my mother,
you are my friend.
That makes me glad!

At times I remember, and reflect on my childhood. It amazes me and humbles me. I understand things better now.

How dear to this heart are the scenes of my childhood, when fond recollection presents them to view.

SAMUEL WOODWORTH

23

Mother's apron gave you assurance. Rushing in from school or play, even if you didn't see or hear her, you felt better just finding that apron hanging behind the kitchen door or dangling across a chair. Her apron, smelling of cookies and starch and Mother. It comforted you. It made you feel secure. It was part of her—like her laugh or her eyes.

MARJORIE HOLMES

My mother's love for
me was so great
that I have worked
hard to justify it.

MARC CHAGALL

*No matter how old we get, it is still
important to make mom proud.*

You were never a perfect mother. I never had to be a perfect kid. Yet the love was always there, each for the other. What a relief to live in reality.

Children find comfort in flaws, ignorance, insecurities similar to their own. I love my mother for letting me see hers.

ERMA BOMBECK

Some are kissing mothers
and some are scolding
mothers, but it is love just
the same, and most
mothers kiss and scold
together.

PEARL S. BUCK

And how wise the mother who
does "scold and kiss together."

Nobody knows of the work it makes

To keep the home together,

Nobody knows of the steps it takes,

Nobody knows—but mother.

ANONYMOUS

29

You have to love your

children unselfishly.

That's hard.

But it's the only way.

BARBARA BUSH

I've known some selfish mothers,
which makes me realize how blessed
I am that mine is not!

A mother is like a veil: she
hides the faults of her children.

YIDDISH PROVERB

Where would I be today,
if not for your ability to look
beyond my faults and visualize
all my pent-up potential?

How great to have a mother
who is not only wise but clever!

An ounce of wisdom is worth

more than tons of cleverness.

BALTASAR GRACIAN

*I don't know how mothers
accomplish all they do.
They probably don't either!*

The word *mother* is
a synonym for some
of the hardest, most
demanding work
ever shouldered
by any human.

LIZ SMITH

A mother understands
what a child does not say.

ANONYMOUS

Even now you seem
to read my thoughts
and feel what my
heart feels, but cannot say.

Time and again I find myself wondering, "What would mother do in this situation?"

What we have learned from others becomes our own by reflection.

RALPH WALDO EMERSON

You taught me how
to live and learn from
the lives of others.

We are wise by

other people's

experience.

SAMUEL
RICHARDSON

Knowledge from books;

wisdom from life.

JEWISH PROVERB

We watch and want to be
the good that we see.

Now thank we all our God,

With hearts, and hands and voices,

Who wondrous things has done,

In whom His world rejoices;

Who from our mother's arms

Has blessed us on our way

With countless gifts of love,

And still is ours today.

MARTIN RINKART

41

The measure
of love is
compassion;
the measure
of compassion
is kindness.

ANONYMOUS

*I'm so touched by your
compassion, which reaches far
beyond our family to so many
who need a touch of kindness.*

Nothing means as
much as my dear
mother's tender touch.

Mothers must model
the tenderness we
need. Our world can't
find it anywhere else.

CHARLES R. SWINDOLL

43

*Rain or shine, mother
of mine, your love was
always there when I
needed it most.*

A noble heart is a

changeless heart.

ANONYMOUS

The memory of a well-spent
life never dies.

CICERO

I cannot keep you forever,
but the memories I can hold
close in my heart.

No woman can be strong,
gentle, pure, and good without
the world being better for it,
without somebody being
helped and comforted
by the very existence
of that goodness.

PHILLIPS BROOKS

*I could fill books with the
names of people who know you
care—and care deeply.*

You taught me to expect the most and believe the best. That gives me courage to face an uncertain future.

Whatever enlarges hope will exalt courage.

SAMUEL JOHNSON

48

That habit of giving only
enhances the desire to give.

WALT WHITMAN

Your generous heart gives out
to others and makes them
want to give back to you.

They're only truly great

who are truly good.

GEORGE CHAPMAN

I think you're great,
because you're a truly
good mom!

The supreme
happiness of life is
the conviction that
we are loved; loved
for ourselves—
rather, loved in
spite of ourselves.

VICTOR HUGO

Who can love us freckles,
phobias, and such . . . but our
blessedly biased mothers?

In the final analysis it is
not what you do for your
children but what you
have taught them to do
for themselves that will
make them successful
human beings.

ANN LANDERS

I've always been glad that you
were never afraid to push me
out of the nest—and that you
waited until I could fly!

*I have no doubt God chuckled
to think of your surprising
personality, and sighed with
contentment to know what a
wonderful mother you'd be.*

When God thought of
Mother, He must have
laughed with satisfaction—
so rich, so deep, so full of
power and beauty was the
conception.

HENRY WARD BEECHER

Mothers are

quintessential people.

ALEXANDRA
STODDARD

Youth fades,
love droops,
the leaves of
friendship fall . . .
a mother's love
outlives them all.

OLIVER WENDELL
HOLMES

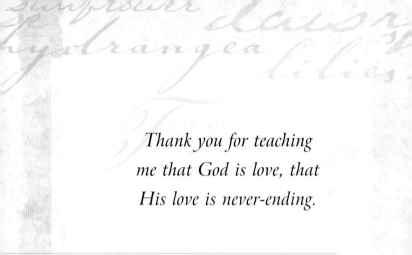

*Thank you for teaching
me that God is love, that
His love is never-ending.*

I remember my mother, my
father and the rest of us praying
together each evening. It is
God's greatest gift to the family.

MOTHER TERESA

Mama was like a flowing
river, blessing the banks
of life around her.

MARGARET JENSEN

Oh, God, for others let me be,
at least half the blessing
my dear Mother has been to me.

You filled my life
with the wealth of
wisdom that comes
from loving God.

No one is poor who
had a godly mother.

ABRAHAM LINCOLN

I certainly don't have to apologize for being one of your most ardent admirers.

A hero is someone we can admire without apology.

KITTY KELLEY

We are in truth,
more than
half what
we are by
imitation. The
great point is,
to choose good
models and to study
them with care.

LORD CHESTERFIELD

Mom, I choose you!

Joy is knowing your
mom loves you,
even (especially)
when you don't
deserve to be loved.

Blessed are

the joy-makers.

NATHANIEL
PARKER WILLIS

62

Hope, like the gleaming taper's light;

adorns and cheers our way.

and still, as darker grows the night,

emits a brighter ray.

OLIVER GOLDSMITH

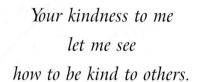

Your kindness to me
let me see
how to be kind to others.

We are made

kind by

being kind.

ERIC HOFFER

How is it you always seem
to know exactly when I
need a glimmer of laughter
to chase away the gloom?

A good laugh

is sunshine in

a house.

WILLIAM
THACKERAY

We learn
only from
those whom
we love.

GOETHE

I'm still learning . . . still loving . . .
so grateful to be loved by you.

The child praises the mother.

The house

praises the

carpenter.

RALPH
WALDO
EMERSON

To serve is
beautiful, but
only if it is
done with joy
and a whole
heart and a
free mind.

PEARL S. BUCK

I can't count the times you
have served others, not
only joyfully but willingly.

When a woman puts
her finger for the first
time into the tiny hand
of her baby and feels
that helpless clutch
that tightens her very
heartstrings, she is
born again with the
newborn child.

KATE DOUGLAS WIGGIN

No one has given more to my
life than you, Mother.

Mother's love grows by giving.

CHARLES LAMB

Everything
I learned
about love,
I learned
from my
mother.

MARITA
GOLDEN

I learned things like
a hug can let you
know you're special.

You made our home a
sanctuary—a haven
from the hectic, harried,
world outside.

The woman
is the heart
of the home.

MOTHER TERESA

There is no greater place
of ministry, position,
or power than that
of a mother.

PHIL WHISENHUNT

God could
use a few
more mothers,
like mine.

75

The wise woman builds her house.

PROVERBS 14:1

*The older I get, the more
I marvel at the work and
determination you poured into
making our house a home, not only
a beautiful home but a godly home.*

There is no more
influential or
powerful role
on earth than
a mother's.

CHARLES R.
SWINDOLL

You have been one of the most
positive and significant influences
in my life. Thank you for being a
wonderful role model.

I honor you mother. Not just for giving me life, but for making my life a gift.

Honor your father and mother, even as you honor God, for all three were partners in your creation.

JEWISH PROVERB

The shepherd always tries to persuade the sheep that their interests and his are the same.

STENDHAL

A mom does the same thing with her kids. Only she has to be more subtle about it.

To love someone more
dearly every day,
To help a wandering child
to find his way,
To ponder o'er a noble
thought and pray,
And smile when evening
falls—this is my task.

MAUDE LOUISE RAY

81

I always seek the good that is in
people and leave the bad to Him
who made mankind and knows
how to round off the corners.

GOETHE'S MOTHER

How glad we can
be that God does
indeed let us leave
the rounding
off to Him.

She who gives all,
though but little,
gives much.

QUARLES

Even when we didn't have much,
you taught us to give generously.
You were teaching us how to open
the door of God's rich blessings not
only for our lives but for others.

Mom, you are truly
one of God's greatest
gifts to me.

I thank God for
my mother as for
no other gift of
His bestowing.

WILLARD

How beautiful
a day can be
when kindness
touches it!

ELLISTON

86

Mothers have big aprons—to cover the faults of their children.

JEWISH PROVERB

Every kid needs a mother's forgiving heart to hide behind.

To be good is noble,
but to show others how
to be good is nobler.

MARK TWAIN

When I didn't listen to the good you said, I couldn't ignore the good you did.

I remember my mother's prayers . . . and they have clung to me all my life.

ABRAHAM LINCOLN

I will always count on your prayers, Mom.

If you were blessed with a good mother, you will reap the benefits all of your days.

CHARLES R. SWINDOLL

Mom, the legacy of your love goes on and on and on.